Tween Kwisine

A Road to Better Health

© 2005 Happy Dog Publications, LLC
All Rights Reserved.

No part of this publication may be reproduced, stored in a retrieval system, or transmitted, in any form or by any means, electronic, mechanical, photocopying, recording, or otherwise, without the written permission of the author.

First published by Dog Ear Publishing
4010 W. 86th Street, Ste H
Indianapolis, IN 46268
www.dogearpublishing.net

ISBN:0-9766603-1-8

This book is printed on acid-free paper.

Printed in the United States of America

Acknowledgements

My sincere appreciation goes to the following people:

Tamara, for inspiring the idea for this book and being my biggest supporter.

Christina who provided me with what's hip for tweens.

Julie Malfitano, who's wonderful illustrations make this book a magical experience.

And, my sister Patricia who seems to think I can accomplish anything.

Special Thanks

A special thank you goes out to all the kids who shared their favorite recipes and enthusiasm for this project, without their input, this would just be another cookbook.

Dedication

To my husband, whose love, support and hard work allowed me to pursue my dreams.

To my dog Kona, who became a permanent fixture in my office and constant companion, and to my other dog Mika who didn't hold it against me.

Table of Content

Acknowledgements i
Introduction to Parents 1
Introduction to Tweens 6
Disclaimer Page 8
A quiz to get you started 10
Some General Words 11
Helpful Kitchen Tips 13
Breakfast 15
Breads & Muffins 32
Lunch 40
Snacks 50
Salads 64
Soup 76
Dinner 80
Sides 96
Desserts 104
Appendix A: Measurement conversions 114
Appendix B: Ingredient Substitution List 118
Index 124
About the Author 130
About the Artist 131
References 132

Happy Dog Publications, LLC
Parker, Colorado
Telephone: 720-851-5297
e-mail: info@happydogpublications.com
happydogpublications.com

Introduction to Parents

Our children are experiencing a serious health crisis. If we do not get educated about it and facilitate change it is estimated that our children will not even live to the current lifespan of adults today. In fact, cancer, diabetes, asthma, obesity, ADHD and degenerative diseases are more prevalent than ever.

One in four children is obese and nearly 50% of children who remain obese as adolescents continue the trend as adults (Int'l Journal of Obesity 1999 & Pediatrics, 1998). By age 3, children have fatty deposits in their arteries and by age twelve, 70% have developed beginning stages of hardening of the arteries (Bogalusa Heart Study NHLBI, 2002).

More than 8 million children have asthma. This statistic has increased 232% over the last 40 years (Archives of Pediatric/Adolescent Medicine, 2000) and 25% of all 12 year olds have higher than normal blood pressure (Berenson, 2004)

Did you know that less than 7% of all school age kids get the recommended 2 servings of fruits and 3 servings of vegetables per day? (Archives of Pediatric/Adolescent medicine, 1996). If ketchup and French fries were not considered the figure would be even less.

Introduction

One of the most significant actions we can take is to improve how and what we eat. It's time to pay more attention and to realize that diet has a major impact on health, longevity and disease control. We can no longer rely on false nutritional support of vitamin supplements, surrender to busy schedules, finicky eaters, fast food, and overwhelming advertisements. It's time to take control AND give some of that control to our kids. By the time our kids reach pre-teen age, they are capable of making some decisions for themselves and taking some responsibility for their own health.

Tween Kwisine: *A Road to Better Health* contains fun, easy and healthful recipes your kids can make from the very kids who are creating them. I am proud to include these recipes as well as some of my own that have been created from my love of cooking healthy food that is also enjoyable to eat. We can win, but it takes some patience, love, education and some creative rights to the kitchen for our kids.

I agonized over including nutritional information such as how much protein, fat, carbohydrate and calories were in each item, but what I concluded was that I wanted the emphasis to be on the nutrition education that is instilled as the kids go through the book. I want Tween Kwisine to focus on qualitative not quantitative nutrition. This means paying attention to the nutrient quality of the foods we are buying and consuming. There is a big difference between quality foods providing the necessary elements we

Introduction

need for good nutrition, and fortified packaged foods that provide a few multivitamins and minerals that have been replaced in unproven quantities and artificially produced. The bottom line is that the key to good nutrition involves moderation not deprivation and above all, education.

I really want Tween Kwisine: *A Road to Better Health* to be a departure from America's obsession with calories, net carbs, and fat content. Our youth today are inundated with unhealthy messages every day from every direction. In fact, the average child receives over 40,000 negative health messages per year. This is definitely having an impact on their health. It also impacts what products are produced and distributed in the marketplace. We have become a nation so focused on carb and calorie numbers on one side, and unhealthy food promotion on the other, that it has spurred an entire artificial food revolution that is out of control.

With all the "designer" food consumed now, it is no wonder that we do not have room for real food in our diets. We are literally a nation of living people consuming mostly dead food.

In light of all the negative health statistics and the recommendations that we consume at least 9 to 13 servings of fruits and vegetables every day (Am. Cancer Society 2004), it may seem as though there is little hope of change. While I believe this book can help make a positive impact on the whole family,

Introduction

we can all use a little more dietary insurance. According to research we are finding that isolated nutrients in the form of vitamins are not the answer. However, in my professional opinion, there is a ray of hope. I have found a product that is so revolutionary it could easily change the state of the world's health. It is called Juice Plus+®. Juice Plus+® is the essence of 17 raw fruits, vegetables and grains in capsules, gummies, and chewable form. Sound too good to be true? It's not. Independent, third party, peer reviewed research is proving it. In fact, Juice Plus+® is the most researched whole food based nutritional product in the world. While it is not a substitute for eating healthy, it can be a catalyst to improvement.

Currently there are over 15 medical institutions and research facilities around the world conducting valid research with Juice Plus+®. There is also an ongoing Children's Research Study worldwide that includes 50,000 participants in 14 countries. Every child that is sponsored by an adult family member receives their product for free for up to 3 years. Preliminary results are extremely significant. After 12 month of use, children on the study experienced a 90% increase in health awareness alone. Other vital statistics show:

58% less school days missed
62% less need for doctor visits
73% less fast food eaten
62% reported eating more fruits and veggies
(NSA, 2004)

Introduction

Overall academic achievement and athletic participation improved dramatically as well. These results are in direct correlation to the incorporation of Juice Plus+® into children's diets. The study has recently received enough funding to continue for 5 more years and expand to 250,000 participants. This will help to confirm and increase statistical significance.

I hope your whole family will enjoy Tween Kwisine: *A Road to Better Health* and learn a little something along the way that will help propel you all into a healthier, stronger future. After all, our kids are our future.

Introduction to Tweens

On the highway of life, there are many roads you can choose to travel. Some roads are better than others and ultimately you are responsible for the choices you make and the roads you choose to follow.

Tween Kwisine is designed to be a roadmap to better health. As you travel through the pages you will learn some things about you, your decision making abilities and your health. You will also encounter traffic signs that will help you down the right roads. The "GO" sign means that this is an excellent road to follow. "CAUTION" means be careful, proceed with care, this road traveled often could have negative consequences.

Tween Kwisine is your very own cookbook to help you create some cool snacks and healthy meals. Best of all, Mom has to let you use the kitchen. As you probably know, fast food, chips and soft drinks are probably not your best choices when it comes to eating. Once in a while it's okay to indulge but for the most part you have to treat your body as if it were your temple. Did you know that most people take better care of their cars than they do their own bodies? If you could drive and needed gas would you simply put water in the tank and expect it to run at peak performance? Of course not, you would put the highest grade fuel in it that you could to make sure it gets you where you need to go without any problems.

Introduction

The same principle applies to your body and what you put in it. In order to get maximum energy and performance, you have to give it the best fuel you can. That's where this book will come in handy. Not only will you be able to make some great food that you like and that you can feel good about eating, but you will learn some stuff about health that you can take with you for the rest of your life and pass on to your kids. After all, if you don't take care of your body, where are you going to live?

Most of the recipes in the book were submitted by kids about your age, with the exception of the one's I added that I thought would compliment theirs. I hope you have lots of fun with this and learn some cool stuff along the way about the roads you want to follow and your creative skills in the kitchen!

Cooking seems to be a dying art for a lot of busy families. Let's bring back the joy of cooking as well as the satisfaction of knowing that you contributed to the health of yourself and your family.

Please visit my website at: www.happydogpublications.com and submit some of your recipes for the next edition. Make sure to include your age (9 to 14) your first name and the city where you live.

Introduction

Disclaimer Page

Since not everyone uses cow's milk, all the recipes that call for milk as an ingredient are interchangeable with whatever milk product your family uses. If the recipe calls for evaporated milk or buttermilk and you don't want to use it, see the substitution list in Appendix B for alternatives.

Since oven temperatures vary, recommended cooking times may vary also. It is advised that the product be checked frequently for doneness.

Altitude may affect time and temperature also. Since every altitude cannot be determined, the times specified for cooking or baking are recommendations only.

Recipes in this book have been modified to be healthier versions of the originals. Although you will notice that there are desserts included that don't appear to be the "healthiest" on the planet, I wanted the emphasis to be on natural wholesome ingredients which in moderation are a much better alternative to the prepackaged, processed snacks and desserts on the market today. If we are realistic we know that our kids love sweet treats. Having said that, the desserts I chose to include reflect that need with ingredients that are natural and that don't include transfat, preservatives or artificial coloring.

Introduction

Throughout the book "GO" and "CAUTION" signs will indicate which foods can be eaten often and which should be eaten in moderation and only occasionally.

Introduction

A Quiz to Get You Started

On a Scale from 1 to 10 how important is your health?_____

Do you think exercise is important for your health____?

How many hours a week are you doing something active_____?

How many hours a week do you spend on computer games and TV_____?

If you eat fast food, how many times per week_____?

Do you eat breakfast_____?

Do you eat at least 5 servings of fruits and vegetables every day____?

Did you know that the American Heart Association recommends we eat at least 9 to 13 servings of fruits and veggies every day_____?

Some General Words

It has been said that we do not have a vitamin deficiency we have a whole food deficiency.

There is power in whole food that can help your body stay strong and healthy. Use it as a roadmap and you will have a much easier time coping with all the changes you will go through while growing into a healthy teenager and adult.

To maintain a healthy diet and understand the values in the text boxes throughout the book, there are a few guidelines to note:
Keep your cholesterol intake at or below 300 mg per day.
Keep your fat intake to 20-30% of your total calories per day.
Keep salt intake to about 1 tsp per day (2400 mg).

Believe it or not, over 70% of your state of health can be attributed to what you put in your mouth and how you live your life. In addition, it's important that you know your body is about 75% water. Your cells need water to function properly. By drinking at least ½ your body weight (in ounces) of good filtered water every day, you can help control your weight, minimize headaches, have clearer skin and even think better. How about that!

Introduction

Helpful Kitchen Tips

- Be sure to measure "level" spoons and cups, don't heap, doing that will probably ruin your recipe.
- Keep work space clean.
- Use knives with respect and never point edges toward yourself (or your friends and family for that matter).
- Make sure you use oven mitts when reaching into the oven.
- Turn all appliances off when you are done with them.
- Wash and put away your tools when you are finished.

By following these simple rules, you will not only be courteous but I bet Mom will be happy to let you back into the kitchen next time you want to create a culinary masterpiece.

NOW LET'S GET COOKING!

Breakfast

Breakfast

Nutrition experts tell us that breakfast is the most important meal of the day and yet it tends to be the most frequently skipped. Breakfast means breaking the fast between when you last ate the day before, until the time you get up in the morning and eat again. Your body needs energy to get going. Your brain needs fuel to work properly and believe it or not, breakfast eaters are less likely to gain weight because it lowers the chance of overeating later in the day. So, even if you are rushed in the morning, you will have a much better day if you have something to eat before you get busy.

The egg is one of nature's best sources of complete protein. This means you do not have to combine it with any other food in order to benefit from its high quality protein. Protein is important for building muscle, repairing tissue and building new cells. It is also rich in vitamin B12 and E which are both very important for healthy cells.

The best quality eggs are those that come from chickens who have been allowed to graze the field for natural food. This is called *free range*. Look for *organic grain fed*, *free range* or *cage free* eggs. These eggs do not come from chickens that are "stressed out" from being in cages with many other chickens, nor have they been fed hormones or antibiotics. You don't need any of that!

So, having said that, here are some Eggceptional recipes for, you got it, the egg!

Breakfast

EggMcposer Muffin
Serves 1

1 egg
1 whole grain English muffin, toasted
1 slice of your favorite cheese
1 veggie sausage patty, cooked

1. Fry egg in nonstick skillet.
2. Top one side of muffin with sausage and the other with slice of cheese.
3. Put back in the toaster oven until cheese is melted.
4. Put fried egg on sausage side, fold and eat.

We should only get about 300 mg. of cholesterol from our diets every day because our livers make a fair amount for us already, yet the restaurant version has 225mg. of cholesterol and 710 mg. of sodium, that's almost 1/3 Daily allowance of salt!

Breakfast

Create Your Own Omelette
Serves 1

3 eggs or ¾ cup egg substitute
1 tsp. butter
¼ cup of your favorite grated cheese
veggies of your choice

Here's where the creativity comes in, add whatever else you like to this recipe.

1. Heat skillet and melt butter, add egg and cook on low heat moving the sides in with a spatula as it cooks so egg on inside of pan can move to the outside and cook more evenly.
2. When egg looks about ½ cooked sprinkle cheese and the other ingredients over half and cover.
3. Continue to cook on very low heat for about another minute or two.
4. When cheese is melted and eggs look cooked, take your spatula and fold the egg only side over the ingredients side and presto, you are a gourmet chef!
5. Top with sour cream or salsa if you like.
6. Enjoy with whole wheat toast or muffins and fruit.

Note: You will notice throughout this book that I recommend using real butter. The best you can do is buy natural organic butter. Using organic butter is a good source of vitamin's A and E. These are fat soluble vitamins that contribute to brain function and immunity. That said, it's a good idea to use it sparingly. You don't need to overdo it to benefit.

Breakfast

Cheese and Veggie Scramble
Serves 2

4 eggs or one cup of egg substitute
1 tsp. butter
1/4 cup chopped onion
1/4 cup chopped tomato
1/2 cup chopped fresh spinach
1/2 cup grated regular or 2% cheddar cheese

1. Whisk eggs in a bowl until fluffy.
2. Melt butter in a frying pan on low heat.
3. Add veggies, increase heat to medium and stir around until tender.
4. Add eggs, stir with spatula until the whole mixture begins to set.
5. Add cheese and stir until melted and eggs are cooked.

Breakfast

UFO's
Serves 1

2 pieces whole wheat, sour dough, or rye toast
2 eggs
2 tsp. butter

1. Melt butter on griddle.
2. Carve out a 2-3 inch hole in the middle of each piece of toast.
3. Place toast on griddle.
4. Crack one egg into each hole.
5. Fry until egg is cooked to your liking.

Voila! Eggs and toast all in one!

Submitted by Valinda age 14, Franktown, CO

Breakfast

Quick & Easy Cottage Cheese Pancakes

6 Servings

3 eggs
1 cup low-fat cottage cheese
1/4 cup milk
1 cup whole grain or oat flour

1. Combine first 3 ingredients in blender.
2. Blend until smooth.
3. Add flour and blend again.
4. Cook pancakes on nonstick or lightly greased griddle until golden.

French Toast

Serves 4

4 - 6 eggs or 1 to 1 1/2 cups egg substitute
2 tsp. cinnamon
1/8 cup sugar
Dash nutmeg
1 tsp. vanilla
1/2 cup milk
8 pieces bread

1. Mix all ingredients together in a shallow bowl, except bread.
2. Dip your favorite bread into mix on both sides.
3. Grill on nonstick pancake griddle until lightly browned.
4. Top with maple syrup, jam or fruit.

Submitted by Christina age 13, San Marcos, CA

Breakfast

Breakfast

Bananas are one of those amazingly well packaged, nutrient dense fruits that nature has provided for our good health. The banana has been a staple for people for thousands of years. Did you know that the banana is the most popular fresh fruit in the United States? It is also one of the few fruits that ripen better after being picked. Americans consume about 25 pounds per person per year, yet they are not grown in the United States. We have to get them from the tropical regions around the world. They contain less water then most other fruit so their carbohydrate content by weight is higher. This makes them the snack of choice for athletes. They help fuel all your activities as well as help keep your body fluids in balance due to their high concentration of potassium.

Bananarama Shake
Serves 1

1 small frozen banana
1 cup milk
1 tsp. vanilla

Pour milk in blender, add frozen banana and vanilla and whirl.

Breakfast

Berry Delight
Serves 1

1/2 cup frozen strawberries, blueberries, raspberries, or blackberries (or mix a few of each)
1 cup milk
1/2 frozen banana
1 pkt. stevia or 2 tsp. sugar, optional

Pour milk in blender, add berries and sugar and whirl.

Berries!
You can't say enough about these little powerhouses. Not only are they versatile and can be added to just about anything, they are packed with a wonderful nutritional punch. While different berries may differ in nutrient content, they are all packed with high quality nutrients which prevent our bodies from breaking down on the cellular level.

Taking in the nutrition from fruits and vegetables can be likened to waxing your bike to prevent it from rusting outside. The natural protective chemicals found in plants prevent a similar result inside your body to keep your cells strong and able to withstand damage. Berries are also good for circulation and great for your eyes, memory and brain. Best of all they are sweet but low in sugar so it's hard to eat too many! So go ahead, indulge often and enjoy all the many health benefits these sweet little treats have to offer.

What is Stevia Anyway and Why is it Better than Sugar?

The Indians of Paraguay have used Stevia for centuries. Europeans learned of Stevia when the Spanish Conquistadors of the sixteenth century sent word to Spain that the natives of South America had used it.

Stevia comes from a shrub native to the northern regions of South America. It is now also grown in Brazil, Uruguay, Central America, the U.S., Israel, Thailand and China. We here in the U.S. simply refer to it as the Stevia plant. It has very potent sweetening properties and can be used instead of sugar for cooking, baking and sweetening pretty much anything in place of sugar or those nasty artificial sweeteners that are used in practically everything processed today. Stevia is completely natural and it doesn't affect blood sugar levels like sugar does, or pollute our bodies like artificial sweeteners do. Plus, you don't need very much, since it is pretty concentrated.

Breakfast

Orange/Banana Cremesickle
Serves 1

1 cup milk
$1/2$ cup orange juice
1 small frozen banana

Put all ingredients in blender and whirl until smooth.

Breakfast

Pumpkin Spice Shake
Serves 1

1 cup milk
1 small frozen banana
1 tsp. pumpkin pie spice

Put all ingredients in blender, whirl and serve.

Breakfast

Yogurt is one of those products that just about anyone can benefit from. Because the process of making yogurt produces the enzyme "lactase," lactose intolerant people can generally eat it. When someone is lactose intolerant, that means they get upset stomachs when they try to drink milk, eat ice cream or consume similar milk products. This is because their body does not produce the enzyme that helps digest it.

Enzymes are "helper" molecules. They help all kinds of reactions occur in our bodies. We produce all kinds of different enzymes that are specific to each of their jobs.

Try this fun experiment. Chew up a saltine cracker and don't swallow it right away, keep it in your mouth. Does it stay salty? Or does it get sweet? This is an example of how enzymes help to start digesting the cracker. The specific enzyme called "amylase" breaks down the starch in the cracker and converts it to sugar. Bet you didn't know that digestion starts in your mouth! That's why your mom tells you to chew your food properly, so you can prepare your stomach for the next step in digestion.

Yogurt is a great source of protein, calcium and riboflavin. You can use plain yogurt instead of sour cream, cream, or mayonnaise in your recipes to make them healthier. Stay away from the presweetened and artificially sweetened varieties when you can. Buy organic and the plain variety and add your own fruit instead.

Breakfast

You Go...YOGO
Serves 1

3/4 cup milk
1 small container plain or vanilla yogurt
1/2 cup frozen fruit of your choice

Put everything in blender and whirl.

Breakfast

Did you know that pineapples don't ripen after you take them home? So, it's important to buy a pineapple that is already ripe. Know how to tell? Smell and firmness are the most reliable. That and a label that says it was jet-shipped from Hawaii. They will be more expensive because they had to buy an airline ticket, but, they will be more likely to be in prime condition than those that came over by boat and/or truck.

Pineapple is a great source of vitamin C. Pineapple has a unique enzyme that can help reduce inflammation inside our bodies. This is called bromelain. It is also known to help digest proteins. Be careful not to add fresh pineapple to yogurt or cottage cheese until right before you eat it, otherwise it will start digesting the protein in these substances and change the consistency and taste.

Try this experiment. Make some Jello. While it is still liquid, separate it into two bowls. Add fresh pineapple to one bowl, leave the other one plain. What happened? What did the bowl with the pineapple do? Gelatin is a protein and the enzyme bromelain will eat it up and prevent your Jello from setting. Heat will kill enzymes like bromelain, so if you try the same experiment with canned pineapple, you won't get the same result. All canned fruit has been heated before canning.

Breakfast

Tropical Delight
Serves 1

2 oz. canned pineapple chunks with juice
1 frozen banana
1 cup milk

Put all ingredients in blender and whirl.

By now you get the idea. Create your own smoothies with some of your favorite items. There's no wrong answer!

Juice Plus +® makes a wonderful meal replacement shake called "Complete" that can be added to any of these smoothies to boost the nutritional value. Check it out!

Breads and Muffins

This can be a great breakfast when you are out of time in the morning, but still need something to get you through until snack time.

Peanut Butter and Banana Toast
Serves 1

2 pieces whole grain toast
1 tbsp. organic peanut butter
1 banana

Spread peanut butter on toast, slice banana on top, fold and go!

Breads and Muffins

Liberty's Favorite Banana Bread
Makes 1 loaf

2 eggs, beaten
$1/2$ cup sugar
$1/2$ cup butter
1 cup low-fat buttermilk
1 tsp. baking soda
1 tsp. baking powder
2 cups whole wheat flour
1 large banana, mashed
Nuts and raisins, optional

1. Combine eggs, sugar, butter, and buttermilk.
2. In separate bowl combine dry ingredients, mix well.
3. Add egg mixture, nuts and/or raisins, and banana to dry ingredients and stir until combined.
4. Pour into greased loaf pan and bake at 350 degrees until toothpick inserted comes out clean, about 40-45 minutes.

Submitted by Liberty age 10, Denver, CO

Breads and Muffins

Oatmeal and Applesauce Coffee Cake
Serves 6-9

1 1/2 cups organic rolled oats
1/2 cup oat flour
3/4 cups whole grain pastry flour
1 tsp. cinnamon
1 tsp. allspice
1 tsp. baking powder
1 tsp. baking soda
1/2 cup firmly packed brown sugar
3/4 cup chopped walnuts or pecans
1 1/3 cups applesauce
1/2 cup milk
1 egg

Topping:
2 tsp. butter, 1 tbsp. brown sugar, 1/4 tsp. cinnamon

1. Preheat oven to 375 degrees.
2. Combine first nine ingredients, set aside.
3. Combine applesauce, egg and milk.
4. Add to dry ingredients and stir together just til moistened.
5. Pour into 8x8 inch baking dish that has been lightly greased.
6. Bake for 25-30 minutes.
7. Melt butter with brown sugar and cinnamon until bubbly.
8. Drizzle over cooled cake.

Breads and Muffins

Quick Peanut Bread
Makes 1 loaf

1 3/4 cup whole grain pastry flour
2 tsp. baking powder
1/2 cup brown sugar
2/3 cup chopped peanuts
2 tbsp. butter
1 egg
1 1/4 cup milk
1/2 cup cranberries or raisins, optional

1. Mix dry ingredients together with nuts, then cut in butter with fork.
2. Beat egg with milk and stir into flour mixture.
3. Pour into lightly greased 9x5x3 inch loaf pan and bake at 350 degrees for about 1 hour.
4. When toothpick comes out clean bread is done.
5. Turn out on cake rack and cool thoroughly before cutting.

Breads and Muffins

Fitness Muffins
Makes 12

1 cup all bran cereal
3/4 cup milk
3/4 cup cinnamon applesauce
2 egg whites
1 1/4 cup whole grain pastry flour
1 1/2 tsp. baking powder
1 1/2 tsp. baking soda
1 tsp. allspice
1 tsp. cinnamon
3/4 cup chopped walnuts, optional

1. Combine milk, cereal, applesauce and egg whites and set aside.
2. Combine dry ingredients in separate bowl.
3. When cereal is softened add to dry ingredients.
4. Stir until mixed, do not over stir.
5. Grease muffin tins and fill each 1/2 way.
6. Bake in preheated 375 degree oven for 15-20 minutes.

Blueberry Hazelnut Muffins
Yields 12

2 cups whole grain pastry flour
3 1/2 tsp. baking powder
1/2 tsp. baking soda
1/4 tsp. nutmeg
1 tsp. cinnamon
2 tbsp. brown sugar
1 egg
1/2 cup nonfat milk
8 ounces vanilla yogurt
1/4 cup applesauce
1 tsp. vanilla
1 cup blueberries
1/2 cup chopped hazelnuts

1. Combine flour, baking powder, baking soda and spices, set aside.
2. Combine sugar, egg, milk, yogurt, applesauce, and vanilla.
3. Add dry ingredients to wet ingredients.
4. Fold in blueberries and nuts.
5. Fill 12 greased muffin cups 1/2 full and bake at 400 degrees for about 10 minutes.

Breads and Muffins

Warp Speed Banana Nut Loaf
Makes 1 loaf

3 very ripe bananas
1/4 cup sugar
1 egg
1 1/2 cup whole grain pastry flour
1/4 cup apple sauce
1 tsp. baking soda
1/4 tsp. salt
1/2 cup chopped walnuts or pecans, optional

1. Mash banana's with fork.
2. Stir in other ingredients.
3. Pour into buttered loaf pan.
4. Bake 1 hour in preheated 325 degree oven.

For a variation on this recipe you can add a 1/2 cup of berries and increase the bake time by 5 to 10 minutes. You will know it's done when you stick a toothpick in the center and it comes out clean.

Submitted by Alyssa age 9, Littleton, CO

Ever checked the label of prepackaged muffins? Do you even know what half those ingredients are? Let alone be able to pronounce them! Let me save you the trouble, there is way too much sugar and too many preservatives and transfat in those babies. Make your own, it's fun and healthy!

Lunch

Easy Pinwheels
Serves 2

2 whole wheat flour tortillas 8 inches in diameter
2 tbsp. mustard
4 slices deli turkey
4 thin slices of provolone cheese (or whatever you like)
1 small carrot, grated
1/4 cup red onion or bell pepper, chopped
4 lettuce leaves, washed and dried

1. Lay out tortillas on clean surface.
2. Spread each with 1 tbsp mustard.
3. Lay 2 slices of turkey and 2 slices of cheese on each tortilla.
4. Sprinkle with carrot and onion and top with lettuce leaf.
5. Starting at one edge, roll tortilla up around filling.
6. Press down firmly to seal edges.
7. Cut each crosswise into 2 pieces.
8. Wrap in foil and refrigerate for later or eat now!

Why go to a fast food restaurant when you can totally make your own! It's not only healthier, it's much cheaper.

Lunch

Vegetarian Wrap
Serves 2

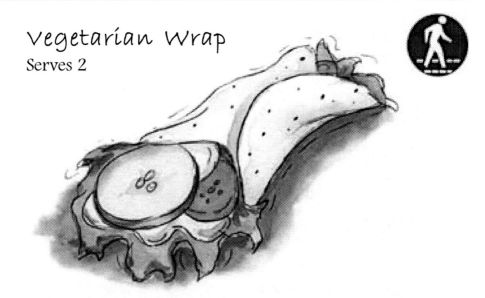

You can add and subtract ingredients according to your own individual tastes. This recipe is so versatile you'll have to keep it handy!

2 whole wheat flour tortillas, 8 inches in diameter
4 tbsp. whipped cream cheese
2 thinly sliced tomatoes
1/2 cup chopped green onion
2 shredded carrots
1/2 cup thinly sliced cucumber

1. Place tortillas on clean surface.
2. Spread each with 2 tbsp. cream cheese.
3. Sprinkle veggies evenly over top.
4. Fold tortilla over and roll up, starting with rounded side closest to you.
5. Place wrap, seam side down, on surface; cut in half diagonally.
6. Wrap in foil and either eat or chill for later.

Lunch

There are over 5 thousand varieties of pears. They have been cultivated for over 4 thousand years and are grown all over the world. They are almost as popular as the apple. Did you know that the pear and apple are actually related? They are both members of the rose family and are classified as "pome" fruits. That means they have a distinct seeded core.

The pear tree was brought to North America by early colonists, who used cuttings from European stock. Pear trees have a very long life span of 75 to 100 years!

Though there are many varieties of pears, the more common ones we see are the Anjou, Bartlett, Bosc and Comice. The Anjou is called the winter pear and isn't quite as sweet tasting as some of the others. The Bartlett is the most popular summer pear. The Bosc is great for baking, it is firm and almost crunchy with reddish brown skin. The Comice has a reputation for being the sweetest and most flavorful pear.

Most of the nutrients like vitamin C are in the skin of the pear so if you buy canned, it will be lower in nutrients not only because it has been cooked but it has also been peeled.

Lunch

Ricotta Pear Broil
Serves 1

1 slice of your favorite bread, toasted
1/4 cup ricotta or cottage cheese
1/2 cup sliced pears
1/8 tsp. cinnamon

1. Spread cheese on toast.
2. Top with fruit and cinnamon.
3. Broil until fruit is hot.

Lunch

Did you know that Americans eat more tuna than any other fish? Only the Japanese eat more. About 95% of the tuna consumed in the U.S. is in canned form unlike Japan where they eat it primarily fresh and raw.

Tuna is a large salt water fish and depending on the type, it can weigh in at almost 1500 pounds! The most common Pacific Ocean tuna are albacore and Yellow Fin. Tuna is primarily known as a great source of complete protein and can be a good alternative to other meats occasionally.

Complete protein means that the food contains all 9 essential *amino acids*, which are protein building blocks. Meat, eggs, fish, cheese, and tofu are good examples of complete proteins.

Tuna Stuffed Pita
Serves 2

1 small can tuna, drained
1 tbsp. organic mayonnaise
1 tbsp. pickle relish
2 tbsp. chopped celery
1 tbsp. chopped tomato
$1/2$ cup alfalfa or broccoli sprouts
1 whole wheat pita sliced in half

1. Mix all ingredients except for the sprouts and pita together in a bowl. (Use more mayo or add some mustard or plain yogurt if it seems too dry).
2. Stuff each side of pita with tuna mixture.
3. Add $1/4$ sprouts to each half.

Ranch / Italian style dressing can be substituted for mayo if you like that better.

Be careful with bottled dressings, they are generally much higher in fat and loaded with preservatives. Try making your own, it's not hard.

Make Your Own Sprouts, It's Easy!

Almost any seed, grain or bean can be sprouted; just make sure the ones you choose are edible. Some examples you can use are lentil, mung, radish, buckwheat, mustard seed and sunflower seeds just to name a few.

1. Rinse the beans, seeds or grains thoroughly and place them in a clean quart-sized glass jar. A quart jar can accommodate up to $1/3$ cup of seed.
2. Fill jar $3/4$ full with tepid water.
3. Cover the mouth of the jar with cheesecloth and secure with a heavy rubber band.
4. Soak, unrefrigerated, overnight.
5. Next morning, drain the beans, seeds or grains well and rinse with fresh water.
6. Rinse and drain well once again, and place the jar lying on its side in a dark area.
7. Rinse and drain the beans, seeds, or grains twice a day, returning the jar to the dark place after each rinsing.

Most seeds will be ready in two to three days. To finish the process, green up the sprouts by placing them in indirect sunlight on the last growing day and then enjoy in your favorite recipe, sandwich or salad. Impressive!

Lunch

Cream Cheese Roll Up.
Serves 1

1 flour or whole wheat tortilla
2 tbsp. lite cream cheese
1/2 cup chopped tomato
1/2 cup sprouts
Enough spinach or lettuce leaves to lay one layer over tortilla.

1. Spread cream cheese on tortilla.
2. Layer spinach or lettuce and sprouts over cheese.
3. Sprinkle chopped tomato over the top.
4. Roll and enjoy!

Okay now you try…….create your own special sandwich or roll up. Remember, the more colorful you make it, the better it is for you!

Color definitely counts on the nutrition scale!

Create your meals as if you were trying to create a rainbow, not only will it be beautiful to look at, your nutritional values will soar as well!

Lunch

Ham and Cheese Burrito
Serves 1

1 flour or whole wheat tortilla
2 slices of your favorite cheese
2 slices lean sandwich ham
Lettuce leaves
1 tbsp. organic mayonnaise
1 tsp. mustard

1. Spread mayo and mustard thinly over tortilla.
2. Lay ham, cheese and lettuce over tortilla to cover it.
3. Roll up and eat!

You should always buy your sandwich meat fresh from the deli, and organic or free range if possible. The prepackaged kind is generally full of preservatives, dyes and salts you don't want or need. But, if you find yourself in front of a package of lunch meat, you can make it somewhat healthier by rinsing it in cold water and patting it dry. This removes most of the preservatives and salts. However, only rinse what you will use right away, otherwise the rest will go bad pretty fast. Buying it fresh is still your better bet.

Personal Pizza
Serves 1

1 whole wheat English muffin
2 tbsp. grated parmesan cheese
1 tbsp. tomato sauce

1. Toast English muffin.
2. Top with tomato sauce and cheese.
3. Broil until cheese is melted.

Try some other variations like adding pineapple, olives, onions or garlic.

Snacks

In terms of snack food, popcorn is one of the nutritional winners, provided you don't pop it in oil and top it with butter. It is high in both complex carbohydrates and fiber. In fact, ounce for ounce, popcorn has about six times the fiber of cooked broccoli and is virtually fat free. Having said that, it is not a substitute for eating veggies just because it is high in fiber content.

Crazy Corn
Makes about 8 cups

8 cups air popped corn
1/3 cup light corn syrup
1/2 cup smooth organic peanut butter
3/4 cup raisins
1/2 cup sunflower seeds

1. Pour popped corn into large bowl.
2. In small saucepan, combine corn syrup and peanut butter, cook over medium heat stirring occasionally so it doesn't burn.
3. When smooth remove from heat (about 5 minutes).
4. Pour mixture over popped corn and stir to coat evenly.
5. Add raisins and sunflower seeds and continue to stir until everything is completely coated.

This is really high in protein, carbs and fiber for a great after school snack that will keep you fueled through your homework!

Checked out movie popcorn lately? Yikes, one large serving of that could easily throw you off the nutritional cliff with fat content! Making your own could very well save you from future clogged arteries, not to mention feeling bloated from all that salt!

Snacks

Easy Cheesy Popcorn

Makes 8 cups

8 cups air popped corn
1/2 cup Parmesan cheese

Pop corn as directed on the package.
Top with Parmesan cheese, enjoy!

Baked Apples

Serves 4

2 apples
1/4 tsp. cinnamon
1 tsp. butter
1 tsp. maple syrup

1. Core apples, leaving 1/2 inch of bottom intact.
2. Place in baking dish.
3. Combine cinnamon, butter and maple syrup.
4. Spoon into center of apples.
5. Cover with foil and bake at 375 degrees for 15-20 minutes or until tender.

Did you know that the 6 most common foods eaten by kids are:

*Pizza
Cookies
White Bread
Chips
Fried Chicken
and Hot Dogs?*

And the 3 most favorite foods are:

*Macaroni and Cheese
Pizza
and Cereal*

Journal of ADA, 1999

Quesadilla

Serves 1

1 burrito size whole wheat tortilla
1/4 cup 2% shredded cheddar or Monterey jack cheese
1/4 cup chopped onions
1/4 cup chopped tomatoes
2 tbsp. salsa
1/2 cup chopped lettuce
Sour cream

1. Heat large skillet.
2. Place tortilla in skillet and warm.
3. Sprinkle cheese, onion, and tomatoes over half the tortilla.
4. Fold tortilla over cheese mixture.
5. Reduce heat, when cheese is melted and tortilla is lightly browned, remove from skillet onto plate.
6. Top with lettuce, salsa and sour cream.

Try substituting vegetarian refried beans in place of the cheese for a leaner version of this favorite or, add the beans and cut down on the cheese for a complete meal.

Snacks

Veggie Bites
Yields 2 cups

1 tbsp. butter, melted
1 egg
1/2 cup whole wheat flour
2 cups of your favorite veggies, cut into bite size pieces
Examples: broccoli, cauliflower, carrots, zucchini, green or red bell pepper

1. Heat oven to 450 degrees.
2. Brush bottom of rectangular pan, 13X9X2, with butter.
3. Dip about 1/4 of the vegetables into egg.
4. Remove 1 vegetable piece at a time with a slotted spoon or fork.
5. Roll in flour to coat and place in pan.
6. Repeat with remaining vegetables.
7. Bake uncovered, turning once, until veggies are crisp-tender and lightly brown, about 10-12 minutes.
8. Sprinkle with grated Parmesan and/or cayenne pepper.

Submitted by Alyssa age 9, Littleton, CO

Bet you thought ordering fried zucchini instead of fries was a healthier alternative. Guess again, one small restaurant serving of these will cost you about 340 calories, ½ of those from fat and about 860 mg of unwanted salt. Baking instead of frying is always going to be your best choice.

Snacks

Next time you reach for a snack keep these statistics in mind, they are part of the reason people are getting sick or overweight when they could avoid it.

Here is the average annual intake of junk food:
60 lbs of cakes and cookies
7 lbs potato chips
23 gallons of ice cream
122 lbs of candy
90 lbs of fat
365 sodas
Journal of ADA, 1999

Yikes!

Did you know that the avocado is actually a fruit? It just has a very large seed. There are over 500 varieties of avocados but we usually only see 2 of them in the stores. The Haas avocado comes from California and has a blackish bumpy skin whereas, the Florida avocado, which is also fondly called the "alligator pear" is bright green with a smooth skin.

The insides are different as well. The Haas avocado is creamy and rich tasting. You can practically spread it like butter. It has more than double the fat and calories of its Florida counterpart. In contrast, the Florida avocado tastes more sweet, nutty and watery because of it.

Most of the fat in these wonderful fruits is monounsaturated, which is good for your heart. Monounsaturated basically means it won't clog your arteries and is good for helping cholesterol levels. It's similar in composition to the fat that is in olive oil.

Bet you didn't know that avocados are also great for your skin and hair!

Snacks

Snacks

Wholey Guacamole!
Makes about 1½ cups

2 med. avocados
½ cup chunky salsa
¼ sour cream, optional

1. Peel, and mash avocados in a bowl with a fork.
2. Add salsa and sour cream.
3 Mix together and serve with chips, veggies or tortillas.

Too many prepackaged convenience foods add up to poor health. Virtually every processed snack food contains artificial colors and flavors, preservatives, flavor enhancers and transfat, yuck!

Snacks

They say an apple a day keeps the doctor away. This could very well be true. Apples are high in fiber, vitamin C and contain over 10,000 different phytonutrients many of which we haven't even identified yet. A phytonutrient is a plant chemical that is beneficial to our health. Scientists haven't quite figured it all out yet, but they have a lot more studies to conduct to see why they are so good for us.

Did you know that there are over 7,500 varieties of apples? The Unites States grows 2,500 varieties alone. Interestingly, only about 8 varieties make up 80% of what we consume. These varieties are more resistant to disease. They ship and store well which explains why they are more abundant.

Some of the best apples for baking and cooking include: Golden Delicious, McIntosh, Granny Smith, Jonathan and Rome Beauty. Others can be used but may not hold a good texture. Experiment with different varieties and see which you like the best. Of course, eating them raw is always going to be the best for your health.

Apple Crisp
Serves 6

6 large apples, cored and cut into 1/2 inch slices
2 tbsp. freshly squeezed lemon juice
1/2 cup raisins
3 tbsp. sugar
2 tbsp. whole grain flour
1 1/2 tsp. cinnamon

Topping:
1/2 cup organic rolled oats
1/2 cup chopped walnuts
1/4 cup brown sugar
3/4 tsp. cinnamon
1 egg, lightly beaten
2 tbsp. vegetable oil

1. Preheat oven to 350 degrees.
2. In large mixing bowl, combine apples, lemon juice, raisins, sugar, flour, and cinnamon.
3. Stir to combine.
4. Place in 9x13 inch baking pan.

Make topping: in medium bowl, combine all ingredients. Spread evenly over fruit mixture. Bake 40 minutes, or until fruit is bubbly.

Snacks

If you've ever bobbed for apples you already know that they float. Do you know why? 20-25% of the volume of raw apples is made up of air located between the cells of the fruit. When you cook them, these cells collapse, forcing the air out, contributing to the soft texture they have after they are cooked. Cool factoid no?

Snacks

Applesauce
Makes 4 cups

3 lbs. apples peeled, cored, seeded and sliced
1/3 cup water
cinnamon, allspice, nutmeg, or ginger to taste

In large pot cook apple slices in water, adding more water only if it dries out before the apples can render their own juices. Cook stirring occasionally until tender, about 15 minutes. Remove from heat and mash with fork or potato masher. Add seasonings to suit your taste. No sugar needed!

Commercial apple sauce can contain up to 77% more calories and sugar than homemade. Also, eating an apple after a meal helps stimulate gum circulation and helps clean your teeth, not a substitute for brushing but a good stand in when you are in a pinch.

Oh, and here's something you may not know. Apple seeds contain a tiny amount of the deadly poison cyanide. Even though you would have to eat hundreds of seeds to have ill effects, it's best not to eat them. So, keep that in mind before you leave your core for a wild animal. Make sure you take out the seeds first since we don't know what effect they might have.

What's wrong with sugar?
No vitamins
No minerals
No enzymes
No amino acids
No fiber
No nutritional value!

Salads

Salads

Sassy Apple Salad
Serves 6

1 egg
1/4 cup sugar
1 tbsp. flour
1 tbsp. apple cider vinegar
4 chopped apples
10 oz. can crushed pineapple (drained)
8 oz. vanilla yogurt
1 cup nuts, your choice (chopped)

1. Whisk egg, sugar, flour and vinegar together and bring to a boil slowly stirring with wire whisk so egg does not harden.
2. Remove from heat and combine with apples and pineapple.
3. Fold in yogurt and nuts.
4. Store in frig for 24 hours before serving.

Did you know that vinegar contains an acid type substance that will help prevent your apples from *oxidizing* (turning brown) Lemon juice will do the same thing. Cool huh?

Sumi Salad
Serves 4-6

1 small bag coleslaw cabbage
3 green onions, chopped
3 tbsp. sesame seeds
1/4 cup sliced almonds

Dressing:
1/4 cup olive oil
3 tbsp. seasoned rice wine vinegar

1. Place cabbage in large salad bowl.
2. Add chopped green onions.
3. Brown sesame seeds and almonds in small non-stick pan.
4. Combine olive oil and rice wine vinegar.
5. When almonds and sesame seeds cool, add to cabbage mixture.
6. Just before serving add dressing and toss.

Salads

California Chicken Salad
Serves 4

6 cups romaine lettuce, washed and dried
1 pound free range boneless, skinless chicken breast, poached or roasted
1 medium shallot, chopped
1/2 cup slivered almonds
1/2 cup croutons
1/2 cup shredded parmesan cheese

1. Make dressing below.
2. In large bowl, tear lettuce into bite-size pieces.
3. Dice chicken breast and add to lettuce.
4. Add shallot, almonds, and croutons.
5. Top with cheese.
6. Toss with dressing, just enough to wet.

Creamy Garlic Dressing:
1 cup plain yogurt
1 1/2 tsp. Dijon or spicy brown mustard
2 cloves garlic, crushed
1/8 tsp. cayenne pepper
1 tsp. olive oil

Whisk all ingredients and refrigerate for 2 hours.

Salads

What's a shallot?

A Shallot is a mild tasting onionlike vegetable. It actually resembles onion and garlic because it is wrapped in an onionlike yellowish or brownish skin but it is divided into small segmented cloves like garlic. Select those that are firm, dry, and free of sprouts. Use them in place of onions to impart a delicate savory flavor.

Salads

Three Bean Salad
Serves 6

1 can (16 oz.) green beans, rinsed and drained
1 can (8 oz.) garbanzo beans, rinsed and drained
1 can (8 oz.) kidney beans, rinsed and drained
1/4 cup chopped red onion

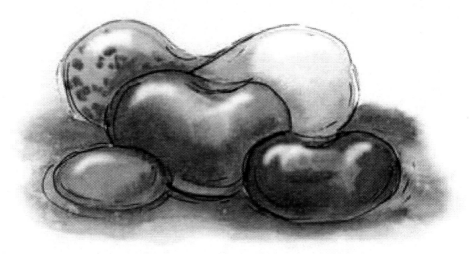

Dressing:
1/4 cup seasoned rice wine vinegar
1/8 cup olive oil
1 tbsp. dried parsley
1/4 tsp. onion powder
1/8 tsp. garlic powder

Mix all ingredients together and toss.

Here is another dish that's packed with great nutrition. Notice the colors, red, orange, green. The more colorful your recipe, the more nutritious it is. Fruits and veggies carry their phytonutrient powers in their skins. The deeper the color the better, because in nature, color is what protects plants from environmental pollutants, UV from the sun, and disease. The neat thing is that when we eat them, we get the same powerful protection.

Chicken, Spinach, and Fruit Salad
Serves 7

8 ounces fresh spinach
2 oranges, peeled and cut into chunks
2 cups cooked and cubed free range chicken breast
2 cups strawberries
1/2 cup sliced almonds, roasted in nonstick frying pan until lightly brown
1 tbsp. Poppy seeds

Dressing:
3 tbsp. apple cider vinegar
3 tbsp. orange juice
1 1/2 tbsp. olive oil
1/4 tsp. dry mustard

1. Combine salad ingredients in large salad bowl.
2. Combine salad dressing ingredients and whisk.
3. Pour dressing over salad right before serving and toss.

Salads

Potatoes can be very nutritious, especially if you keep the skins on because most of the best nutrients are right under the skin. Plus, the skin provides a good source of fiber. In fact, the potato may have changed the course of history.

The potato was first brought to Europe from South America around 1570. It provided much needed calories and nutrients to the diet of the poor, particularly in Ireland. Dependence on the potato in that country became so great that when the crop failed in the 1840's, it led to widespread famine and massive emigration to the United States.

Today, the potato is the most widely consumed and economically important vegetable in the world. The United States alone produces about 35 billion pounds of potatoes annually and the average American consumes about 126 pounds per person per year.

Potatoes are grown underground so they are members of the "nightshade" family. They are referred to as a tuber not a root and are a good source of many minerals and vitamin C.

Herbed Potato Salad

Serves 6

1 lb. new red potatoes
1/2 cup sliced radishes and onion, optional
Dressing:
3 tbsp. nonfat plain yogurt
1 tbsp. reduced or fat free organic mayonnaise
1 1/2 tsp. Dijon mustard
1/2 tsp. chopped garlic
1/2 tsp. dried basil
1/4 tsp. dried thyme
1/4 tsp. onion powder

1. Scrub potatoes and cube.
2. Place in medium saucepan and cover with water.
3. Bring to boil, cover and reduce heat to simmer for about 12 minutes or until "fork" tender.
4. Drain.
5. Mix dressing ingredients.
6. Combine potatoes with dressing and toss.

You can serve this warm or cold.

Salads

Lentils and colorful veggies together are a powerful combination packed full of antioxidants. This combo combines complex carbohyrates, protein, and fiber from the lentils and veggies and rice to keep you fueled from stem to stern! Here's something you probably didn't know; the peanut is actually a legume, not a nut!

Lentil & Rice Salad
Serves 7

1/2 cup lentils
1 1/2 cups water
1 cup chopped tomato
1/2 cup sliced green onion
1 cup diced carrots
1/2 cup chopped green pepper
1/2 cup chopped red pepper
1 cup broccoli flowerets
1 tbsp. dried parsley
3/4 cup brown rice

Salads

Dressing:

3 tbsp. seasoned rice wine vinegar

1 tbsp. lemon juice

1 1/2 tsp. Dijon mustard

1. Add lentils to water in a medium saucepan and bring to a boil.
2. Reduce heat, cover and simmer for 20 minutes. Drain.
3. Cook rice according to package directions.
4. Prepare vegetables while lentils are cooking.
5. Mix lentils, rice and vegetables.
6. Mix dressing ingredients and pour over vegetable mixture.
7. Chill well before serving.

Making your own dressing will save on artificial colors and preservatives, and, you can control the fat and calories which is what can turn a salad into an unhealthy choice. I don't recommend fat free bottled dressings either as there are way too many artificial ingredients in them that the body does not understand.

Bailey's Grilled Salmon Caesar Salad

Serves 3

1 lb. wild Alaskan salmon
1 head romaine lettuce
4 slices bread of your choice, cubed
2 tsp. garlic powder
1 tbsp. olive oil

1. Grill or broil salmon until done (ask mom or dad to help you with this).
2. Wash, dry and tear lettuce into bite size pieces and put in large serving bowl.
3. Toss cubed bread with garlic powder and olive oil.
4. Brown cubes in oven at 350 degrees for about 20 minutes or until golden brown, turn them over to brown evenly after 10 minutes.
5. Set aside.

Unlike real eggs, you don't need to worry about using egg substitute because it is pasteurized which means that the bacteria that would cause salmonella has been destroyed by heat.

Dressing:
- 1/8 cup egg substitute
- Dash worchestershire sauce
- 1 squeeze lemon
- 4 tbsp. parmesan cheese
- 4 cloves garlic, crushed
- 1/2 cup olive oil
- Fresh cracked pepper to taste.

1. Whisk all dressing ingredients together.
2. Add cooked salmon and croutons to lettuce.
3. Pour dressing onto salad and toss.

Serve with freshly grated parmesan cheese and warm crusty bread.

Submitted by Bailey age 10, Parker, CO

Salmon is one of those essential foods that provide an excellent source of protein as well as heart healthy omega 3 fatty acids. We need omega 3's in our diet to keep our circulatory and nervous systems healthy. It is also something most people don't get enough of. Omega 3 is also found in abundance in ground flax seed, flax seed oil and other fatty fish like mackerel.

Soups

Pumpkin is a great source of antioxidants, vitamin A, potassium and vitamin C, and it makes more than a great pie, it makes a great healthy Fall soup!

Creamy Pumpkin Soup
Serves 4

2 tbsp. butter
1 lg. onion, minced
2 cups low sodium chicken broth
1 cup milk
2 tbsp. cream cheese
1 can (15 oz.) pureed pumpkin
1 tsp. nutmeg or pumpkin pie spice
Salt and pepper to taste

1. In large saucepan, melt butter and cook onion until soft.
2. In separate bowl, mix cream cheese, pumpkin, broth, milk and nutmeg.
3. Heat until cream cheese is melted and it looks creamy.
4. Add to onion mixture.
5. Put soup in blender and whirl until smooth.
6. Pour back into saucepan and simmer for 20 minutes.

Soups

Christina's Basic Chicken Noodle Soup

Serves 5

1 Qt. free range, fat free chicken broth
2 cups whole wheat pasta noodles

1. In large saucepan, bring chicken broth to a boil.
2. Add pasta and cook until done and serve.

This recipe is so versatile you can add anything else you would like, such as carrots, celery, squash and/or onions. Yummy!

Submitted by Christina age 13, San Marcos, CA

Do you think freeze dried packaged noodle soup mix is a healthy snack or meal? Ever looked at the contents label? Forget it! One package made to specifications using the seasoning mix will cost you 1020mg of salt! I'd say stick with Christina.

Soups

Beans are one of those neat foods that can be classified as carbohydrates AND proteins. They are truly a perfect food. They are high in fiber, they help lower cholesterol, they are virtually fat free and they help keep your digestive tract healthy.

Easy Black Bean Soup
Serves 2

1 can (19 oz.) black beans, undrained
1 1/4 cups frozen corn
1/2 cup salsa
1/2 cup water
2 tsp. lime juice
1/2 tsp. chili powder
1 tsp. ground cumin
1/2 tsp. cayenne pepper
Salt and pepper to taste
1/2 cup shredded cheddar cheese
1/2 cup sour cream optional

1. In medium saucepan combine beans, corn, salsa, water, lime juice, chili powder, cumin, cayenne salt and pepper.
2. Cover, and bring to boil over medium-high heat.
3. Reduce heat and let simmer uncovered for 5 minutes or until bubbly. Serve with cheese and/or sour cream on top.

Soups

Mom's Hearty Split Pea Soup
Serves 6

2 quarts filtered water
1 bag split peas, rinsed and drained
1 onion, diced
6-8 organic carrots, sliced
4 veggie dogs, sliced or 1/2 lb. organic soup meat
1-2 tbsp. chicken broth granules or 4 boullion cubes
Garlic salt to taste

1. Bring water and peas to a boil.
2. Add onion, carrots, meat and broth granules.
3. Simmer about 4 hours, stirring occasially.
4. Add garlic salt to taste.

Dinner

Lightning Speed, Seems Like You Cooked all Day, 5 Can Chili
Serves 8

1- 15 oz. can black beans, drained and rinsed
1- 15 oz. can pinto beans, drained and rinsed
1- 15 oz. can kidney beans, drained and rinsed
1- 15 oz. can chili beans, not drained or rinsed!
1- 28 oz. can diced tomatoes
1 red onion, finely chopped
2 tbsp. brown sugar
1 tbsp. cayenne pepper (more or less depending on how hot you want it)

Combine all ingredients, stir and simmer until bubbly. Serve with cornbread and top with sour cream and/or grated cheddar cheese.

Note: Draining and rinsing canned vegetables and beans helps remove the preservatives and salts you don't want to eat. Make sure to run cold water over them for about 2 minutes. This will remove over 75% of the salts.

If you are really motivated you can cook all your own beans from scratch. Just cook them a day before according to package directions. And, for those of you who have *gastric distress* from beans, *you know what I'm talking about*, soaking them overnight and then rinsing them several times before cooking will reduce the gas producing properties of beans.

Taco Chile

Serves 4-5

½ lb. ground organic turkey breast
1 med. Onion, chopped
1 can (8 oz.) tomato sauce
1 can (16 oz.) diced tomatoes
1 can (16 oz.) pinto or chili beans, undrained
¼ pkg. taco seasoning
½ cup shredded jack or cheddar cheese

1. Brown meat with onion in nonstick stockpot.
2. Add remaining ingredients and simmer for 30 minutes.
3. Top with cheese if desired and serve with warm corn tortillas.

Have you ever read the ingredients label on canned soup? It's enough to steer you clear. Canned soup can have more than ½ your daily salt intake allowance in it, often topping over 1200mg per can!

Tofu is a creamy white soy product made somewhat the same way cheese is produced. It is very bland but its best attribute is that it can pose as anything you want it to. Not only is it low in fat and high in protein, you can eat it cold, grilled, baked, sautéed, or stir-fried. It will take on the flavors you are using in your recipe. Use it as a meat replacement anytime you want to eat light and vegetarian.

If you eat soy products like Tempe, tofu, miso and edamame you will get complete protein in vegetable form. If you've never tried it, give it a go. Try the following recipe.

Tofu and Veggie Stir-Fry
Serves 4

1 bag fresh stir fry veggies
16 oz. container firm tofu
2 cloves garlic, peeled and chopped
2 tbsp. low sodium soy sauce
1 tbsp. brown sugar
1 tsp. sesame oil
1 tsp. crushed red peppers
1 tsp. cornstarch
1 tbsp. vegetable oil

Dinner

1. Mix soy sauce, brown sugar, sesame oil, cornstarch and crushed red pepper, set aside.
2. Stir fry veggies in the vegetable oil (be careful not to get oil too hot).
3. Add garlic and cook another 2 minutes.
4. Cut tofu into cubes and add to veggies.
5. Add sauce mixture and heat until bubbly and thickened.

Serve with brown rice or whole grain pasta made according to package directions.

For a heartier version you can stir-fry some cubed beef or chicken. If you like beef, make sure to buy grass fed beef that doesn't come from big production farms. This ensures maximum nutritional value as well as beef that hasn't been injected with antibiotics and growth hormones. Beef can actually be a healthy food if you pay attention to detail.

Sawyer's Shrimp Scampi
Serves 4

2 lbs. shrimp, peeled and deveined
1/2 cup butter
1 tsp. lemon pepper
1/2 tsp. garlic salt and garlic powder

1. Spray a nonstick pan with cooking spray or put small amount of olive oil in pan to coat entire pan.
2. Heat on medium.
3. When a drop of water sizzles on pan, add shrimp.
4. Cook shrimp quickly turning once until pink on both sides.
   Note: don't let oil in pan smoke, keep heat on low to medium.
5. Melt butter in large pan.
6. Add seasonings.
7. When shrimp is done, add to melted butter mixture.
8. Cook 8 ounces of your favorite pasta according to package directions.
9. Drain pasta and serve shrimp mixture over top of pasta.

Your family with think you have turned into a professional chef!

Submitted by Sawyer age 11, Escondido, CA

Italian Tomato and Basil Pasta
Serves 4

6 Roma tomatoes, diced
2 tsp. dried basil
2 cloves garlic, chopped
1/4 tsp. salt
1/8 tsp. pepper
2 tbsp. extra virgin cold pressed olive oil
6 ounces angel hair pasta
Parmesan cheese, optional

1. Mix first 6 ingredients together, cover and let sit at room temp. for at least 1 hour.
2. Cook pasta according to package directions, omitting salt and oil.
3. Drain pasta.
4. Add tomato mixture and toss.
5. Top with parmesan and serve immediately.

Dinner

Fettuccini Alfredo
Serves 4

2 tbsp. butter
1 tbsp. garlic powder
1 1/2 tbsp. flour
12 ounces heavy whipping cream
1/2 cup fresh grated parmesan
1/4 tsp. pepper

1. Melt butter in 2qt. saucepan.
2. With whisk, slowly add the flour and garlic powder making sure there are no lumps.
3. Slowly add whipping cream.
4. Add cheese and stir until melted.
5. Add pepper.
6. Cook fettuccini noodles according to package directions, drain.
7. Toss pasta with sauce and serve.

Manga!

Submitted by Sawyer age 11, Escondido, CA

This recipe is definitely tasty, but should be reserved for those special occasion type meals. Because of the high fat content of this one, it has been lovingly referred to as a "heart attack on a plate". Again, here I think, moderation not deprivation however, if you like having your cake and eating it too, the lighter version of this favorite on the following page can be substituted on a more frequent basis. But that doesn't mean you can't indulge in Sawyer's recipe once in awhile, it would be a shame not to!

Dinner

Fettuccini Alfredo on the Lighter Side

Serves 4

2 tbsp. butter
1-2 tbsp. garlic powder
1-2 tbsp. flour
1 1/3 cup milk
2 tbsp. cream cheese
1 1/4 cup grated fresh parmesan cheese
4 cups cooked fettuccini

1. Melt butter in saucepan over medium heat.
2. Add garlic powder; stir until smooth.
3. Stir in flour with whisk.
4. Gradually add milk, stirring with whisk until blended.
5. Cook until thickened and bubbly, stirring constantly.
6. Stir in cream cheese.
7. Cook about 2 minutes.
8. Add parmesan cheese stirring constantly until melted.
9. Toss with pasta, add pepper.

Crunchy Chicken Nuggets

Serves 4

2 1/2 cups cornflakes
1/2 cup grated parmesan cheese
1/2 tsp. salt
1/2 tsp. onion powder
1/4 tsp. garlic powder
1/8 tsp. pepper
1 lb. Skinless, boneless, grain fed, free range chicken breast strips
1/4 cup flour
1/2 cup egg substitute

1. Preheat oven to 425 degrees.
2. Coat baking sheet with nonstick cooking spray or use nonstick baking sheet.
3. Crush cornflakes in resealable plastic bag with rolling pin or heel of your hand.
4. Pour into shallow bowl.
5. Add parmesan, salt, onion and garlic powder and pepper.
6. Coat chicken in flour.
7. Dip into egg.
8. Roll chicken in cornflake mixture.
9. Arrange chicken in single layer on baking sheet and bake 12-15 minutes until golden brown.
10. Dip into your favorite sauce.

Dinner

Make sure to wash your hands thoroughly after handling raw chicken and clean all surfaces the chicken touched with a good nontoxic kitchen disinfectant. Ask Mom to help you find the right product.

Just 6 little chicken nuggets from a fast food chain will contain over 50% of its calories from fat, since they are deep fried in hot oil. In addition, they contribute at least 330 mg. of salt, 40 mg of cholesterol and almost 300 calories.

Dinner

Dinner

Crock Pot Mushroom Chicken
Serves 4

1 lb. free range chicken thighs or breast, skinned
1 can "Healthy Request" condensed cream of mushroom soup
1 cup plain yogurt
1/2 tsp. paprika
1/4 tsp. Pepper

1. Brown chicken in large skillet.
2. Add mushroom soup, yogurt and spices to crock pot and stir to mix.
3. Place chicken into crock pot.
4. Cover and cook on low for 4 hours.
5. Serve over steamed brown rice.

Submitted by Patty age 14, Denver, CO

Buying meat can be tricky because you want to get the best quality for your money. Make sure the chicken you buy has been grain fed and free range. That means they have been allowed to graze and have not been raised in cages. Check the label also to see if the chicken has been injected with any kind of "flavor enhancing" broth. You want your chicken to be as natural as possible to ensure the best quality meat for you and your family. This will probably cost a bit more money, but will promote a healthier diet and the growth of healthier cells.

Did you know that chiles and peppers are chocked full of vitamin C and a chemical compound called capsaicin (pronounced capsaysin)? Capsaicin works as an anticoagulant. That means it helps keep our blood flowing freely and helps keep it free from clots. These little dynamo's have disease fighting compounds and some say the hotter they are the better they are for you! Typically Poblano peppers are used for chile relleno's and are roasted before canning to give them a more mild flavor.

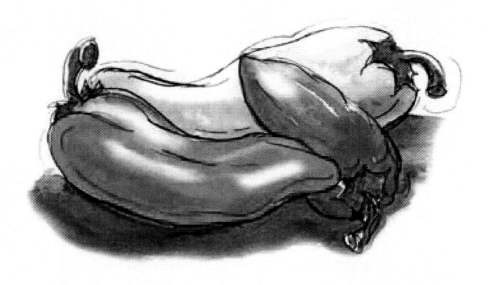

Chile Relleno Casserole
Serves 8

5 - 4 oz. cans diced green chile's
6 - 8 inch whole wheat flour tortillas cut into 1 inch strips
16 ounces grated 2% cheddar or Monterey jack cheese
3 cups egg substitute
Salsa and sour cream optional

1. Preheat oven to 350 degrees.
2. Lightly grease 9x13 inch pan with butter.
3. Lay half the tortilla strips on bottom of pan.
4. Spread 1/2 the chiles over tortillas.
5. Sprinkle 1/2 the cheese over chiles.
4. Repeat another layer.
7. Pour egg substitute over casserole.
8. Bake uncovered for 40 minutes or until puffy and done in the center.
9. Let stand 10 minutes before serving.
10. Top with salsa and/or sour cream if desired.

Serve this one with a side of fruit or salad and some crusty whole grain bread.

Dinner

Zucchini are one of those really easy vegetables to grow in your own garden. They belong to the squash family which also includes melons and cucumber. Squash helped sustain Native Americans for over 5000 years and then helped nourish the early European settlers, who quickly made it a mainstay of their diet. New England colonists adapted the word squash from a variety of Native American names for the vegetable, all of which meant "something eaten raw" although they too ate it cooked.

Zesty Zucchini Frittata

Serves 4

4 cups unpeeled, grated zucchini (about 1½ lbs.)
½ cup chopped onion
2 cloves garlic, minced
6 eggs or 1½ cup egg substitute
2 tbsp. milk
1 tsp. Italian seasoning
¼ tsp. pepper
¼ tsp. garlic salt
½ cup parmesan cheese

1. Lightly grease a 10 inch skillet.
2. Sauté zucchini, onion and garlic until zucchini is tender, pouring off any liquid.
3. Mix eggs, milk and seasonings.
4. Add to zucchini mixture and cook until eggs begin to set.
5. Top with parmesan cheese.
6. Pour entire mixture into lightly greased 8X8 baking dish.
7. Broil until top is lightly golden, 3 to 5 minutes.

Sides

We already know apples are good for us, couple them with sweet potatoes and garlic and you get a great tasting nutritional punch! Sweet potatoes often take a backseat to other potatoes, which is a pity, since they are packed with beta carotene, vitamin's B and C. They have a natural sweetness to them and yet they provide less of a sugar reaction in those that are sensitive than a regular potato does. They are also high in fiber.

The Sweet potato is not related to the white potato, but is a member of the "morning glory" family. It is a Native American plant which was carried to Europe by Columbus and carried to Asia by other explorers. It became the most important means of sustenance for early homesteaders and for soldiers during the Revolutionary War.

Sweet Potato, Garlic and Apple Skillet

Serves about 4

*2 medium sweet potatoes, bake at 375 degrees until soft with skin left on
2 small apples, cubed and cored
2 cloves garlic, minced
1/3 cup walnuts
2 tbsp. olive oil

1. Heat olive oil in skillet.
2. When sweet potatoes are cooled, slice and add to skillet.
3. Add apples and garlic and cook until apples are crisp tender.
4. Add walnuts, toss and serve.

*Be sure you prick your sweet potatoes a couple of times with a fork before baking, this allows air to escape during cooking so they don't explode in your oven.

Garlic

Believe it or not, there is probably more folklore surrounding garlic than any other food. In ancient times it was said to give strength and courage to those who ate it. Egyptians fed it to the slaves who were building the pyramids while Romans gave it to their soldiers and workers. And, in India and China, garlic has been used to ward off evil spirits and was believed to cure everything from broken bones to the common cold. While there is no doubt that garlic has health benefits, we don't yet know all there is to know about it. We do know it seems to contain a chemical that helps keep your blood from clotting and may help lower blood cholesterol.

Sides

Believe it or not, potatoes are not our enemy. It's how we prepare them and what we put on them that are usually the problem. Potatoes are a good source of potassium which is a chemical we need to regulate our body fluids and help keep blood pressure regulated. In fact, half a baked potato with skin on has more potassium than a 6 ounce glass of orange juice. It has anticancer properties and is high in fiber, iron, calcium, phosphorus, zinc, and B vitamins if skin is left on.

Note: Eat potatoes with skin as often as possible except if it has a green tinge to it. This is chlorophyll which isn't harmful in itself but can have toxic properties if eaten under the skin of the potato.

Everyone loves French Fries but we always hear about how bad they are for us. I have a secret recipe that will put the French back into French fry! Enjoy!

No Guilt French Fries
Serves 4

4 potatoes, washed (don't peel them for maximum nutrients)
1/4 cup butter melted

1. Cut each potato in half around the middle.
2. Using mom's apple corer, place potato cut side down and press down with the apple corer to make slices, or slice by hand.
3. Arrange slices on nonstick baking sheet.
4. Using a basting brush, coat all the potato slices with some butter.
5. Bake in preheated 400 degree oven for about 35 to 45 minutes until brown and crispy, turning them once after about 20 minutes.

For a twist on the original, sprinkle some garlic salt or cayenne over the potatoes after basting with butter, Yum!

Make sure you use oven mitts when removing cookie sheet from oven to turn the potatoes over.

Want your French Fries and eat them too? This recipe allows you just that. One serving of regular French Fries from a fast food chain will cost you about 300 calories, almost ½ of those from fat and over 170 mg. of salt. It's amazing what some small changes can accomplish!

Sides

Stuffed Cheesy Potatoes
Serves 8

4 medium russet potatoes, baked
1 cup low-fat cottage or ricotta cheese
1/2 cup parmesan or cheddar cheese, grated
4 tbsp. green onion
1 egg, beaten
1/2 cup low-fat sour cream
1/2 tsp. Paprika

1. Cut each potato in half, lengthwise.
2. Scoop out pulp, leaving about 1/4 inch inside potato skin to make a boat.
3. Blend cheeses, onion, egg and sour cream together.
4. Add potato and mix til smooth.
5. Fill each potato shell half with mixture.
6. Arrange on baking dish and sprinkle with paprika.
7. Preheat oven to 350 degrees.
8. Bake for 15-20 minutes or until heated through.

There's no comparison between this healthy version of the stuffed potato and the restaurant or fast food version which will cost you anywhere from 950 to 1700 mg of salt and way too many saturated fat calories!

Sides

Quick Herbed Rice
Serves 4

2 tsp. instant low-sodium beef, veggie or chicken bouillon
2 cups water
1 tsp. Italian herb seasoning
1/4 cup chopped onion
1 cup brown rice

1. Mix first 4 ingredients together and bring to a boil in a medium saucepan.
2. Add rice and reduce heat to low.
3. Cover and simmer according to package directions.

Here again, anytime you can stay away from the prepackaged versions of this, you save on artificial ingredients, preservatives and lots of salt.

Sides

Red, Yellow and Green Veggie Medley

Serves 4

3 medium zucchini squash, sliced
3 medium yellow squash, sliced
3 Roma tomatoes, sliced
3 cloves of garlic, peeled and sliced
2 tbsp. olive oil

1. Heat olive oil in large skillet.
2. Add zucchini and yellow squash and stir-fry 2 minutes.
3. Add tomato and garlic slices and stir-fry 1 more minute.
4. Serve with chicken, fish or meat.

Color, color and more color! The best way to eat these is with the skin on. Most of the nutritional value is found in the skin and just underneath. Of course, tomatoes are a wonderful source of vitamin C and unlike many veggies, cooking brings out the best in them.

It's estimated that the average kid gets over 40% of their calories from fat!

Garlic Toast
Serves 4

4 slices bread
Butter, garlic salt, parmesan cheese to taste

1. Toast bread.
2. Spread butter over toast lightly.
3. Sprinkle garlic salt and parmesan cheese over top.
4. Serve.

Submitted by Christina 13, San Marcos, CA

Desserts

Now this one may not be the lowest fat dessert you ever eat, however, it is all natural with only 3 understandable ingredients. Take a look at an ice cream container at the grocery store and read the ingredients, can it say the same? Simple and natural far outweighs complicated and unnatural. What do you think?

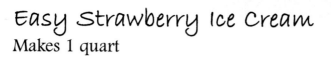

Easy Strawberry Ice Cream
Makes 1 quart

24 ounces frozen strawberries
1/2 cup sugar
1 1/2 cups heavy cream

1. Place berries in blender.
2. Whisk sugar into cream.
3. With blender going, slowly add cream through opening in lid, stopping to stir the mixture 3 or 4 times during the process so ice cream remains smooth.
4. Transfer to shallow glass pan and freeze to a scoopable texture, about 2 hours.

Dessert

Pumpkin Cookies
Makes about 3 dozen

4 cups whole wheat flour
2 cups old fashioned rolled oats, uncooked
1 tsp. baking soda
2 tsp. ground cinnamon
1 1/2 cups butter, softened
1 cup brown sugar
1/2 cup sugar
1 egg
1 tsp. vanilla extract
1 can (16 oz.) pumpkin
Raisins, nuts or chocolate chips, optional

1. Preheat oven to 350 degrees.
2. Lightly grease cookie sheet.
3. Combine flour, oats, baking soda and cinnamon.
4. In separate bowl, combine butter, brown sugar, sugar, egg, vanilla and pumpkin, beat with mixer until smooth.
5. Add in dry ingredients and mix.
6. Spoon onto cookie sheet and bake until firm and lightly brown, about 10-20 minutes depending on how big you make them.

Submitted by Summer age 11, Denver, CO

Everyone loves chocolate, so I had to add just a little! This one is virtually fat free and eggless. It has a significant amount of real cocoa, which does have antioxidants, so, eaten sparingly it can be a healthier alternative to prepackaged cakes.

Be cautious of your choices though when it comes to chocolate. Commercial chocolate syrup for example, is so loaded with sugar it virtually loses any benefit you could have had. Unsweetened cocoa powder is where you will find the antioxidant benefits in chocolate.

Antioxidants are chemicals that help keep your cells from damage.

That said, when looking for a chocolate bar, it is best to get the highest percentage of pure cocoa you can get, 75-85% is not unreasonable. Dark bars are also more likely to have a higher cocoa content while milk chocolate has almost none.

Dessert

Dessert

Wonderfully Chocolate Cake
Serves 16

1 1/4 cups sugar
3 cups whole grain pastry flour
1 cup baking cocoa powder
2 tsp. baking soda
2 tbsp. vinegar
2/3 cup apple sauce
2 tsp. vanilla
2 cups cold water

1. Preheat oven to 350 degrees.
2. Mix first 4 ingredients.
3. Add remainder of ingredients and mix til smooth.
4. Pour into 9X13 inch pan that has been lightly greased.
5. Bake for about 25 minutes.

If making cupcakes decrease baking time to 15 -20 minutes.

Yields about 24

You can top this one or have it plain, either way you will get your chocolate fix and not have to feel too guilty about it!

Dessert

Optional toppings include:
Powdered sugar
Whipped cream
*Chocolate glaze
*Cream glaze

*Chocolate Glaze
Makes about 2/3 cup or 16 servings

1/4 cup milk
1 cup powdered sugar
1 1/2 tbsp. cocoa powder
1/2 tsp. vanilla extract

1. Mix all ingredients and let sit for a few minutes to dissolve sugar.
2. stir and spread lightly over cake.

*Cream Glaze
Makes about 2/3 cup or 16 servings.

This one is very versatile. Experiment with different extracts to create your very own flavor! Try using peppermint or orange extract, there is no end to the possibilities.

1/4 cup milk
1 cup powdered sugar
1/2 tsp. extract of choice

1. Mix all ingredients and let sit for a few minutes to dissolve sugar.
2. Stir and spread lightly over cake.

Dessert

Now I'll bet most of you have never had a pineapple cake before! This very moist cake does not have any fat in it at all, and, it's great all by itself.

Hawaiian Pineapple Cake
Serves 16

1 can (20 oz.) unsweetened crushed pineapple, in juice (not drained)
2 cups whole wheat pastry flour
$2/3$ cup sugar
2 tsp. baking soda
$1/2$ cup egg substitute

1. Preheat oven to 350 degrees.
2. Mix all ingredients and pour ito a 7X11 inch pan that has been lightly greased.
3. Bake for 30-35 minutes.

If you insist on topping this one, you can make this lighter version of Cream Cheese Topping.

Lite Cream Cheese topping
Makes about 4 cups

1 small box (yielding 4 1/2 cup servings) vanilla or white chocolate instant pudding
2 cups milk
6 ounces light cream cheese, room temperature

1. In small mixing bowl combine pudding mix and milk.
2. Beat on low speed to mix well.
3. Add cream cheese.
4. Increase speed and mix until smooth and thick.

Hint: If you are planning to use the topping you can cut the sugar to 1/2 cup in the cake recipe.

Dessert

You can't say enough good stuff about pumpkin, and as far as pie goes, this one is probably on the healthier side of the spectrum. Pumpkin is full of beta carotene, which converts to vitamin A in our bodies when we eat it. Orange, yellow and dark green fruits and veggies have this property in common. The darker the color, the more beta carotene. The wonderful thing about beta carotene is that our bodies are smart enough to know how much they need to convert to keep us healthy and fight cancer and disease. Unlike high doses of vitamin A supplements which can be very dangerous and toxic because they are not natural and the body does not know how to process them properly. Beta carotene in food form is nontoxic even in large amounts. The worst it could do is turn your skin a bit orange if you ate too much over time. For most of us, that probably isn't going to happen.

Dessert

Good Old Pumpkin Pie
Serves 8

³/₄ cup sugar
2 tsp. pumpkin pie spice
2 eggs
1- 15 oz. can pumpkin
1 can skim evaporated milk
1 unbaked 9 inch deep dish pie shell

Note: if you substitute a graham cracker crust for the original you will significantly reduce the fat and calories of this one

1. Mix sugar and pumpkin pie spice in small bowl.
2. Beat eggs in large bowl.
3. Stir in pumpkin and sugar spice mixture.
4. Gradually whip in evaporated milk.
5. Pour into pie shell.
6. Bake in preheated 425 degree oven for 15 minutes.
7. Reduce temperature to 350 degrees and bake 40-50 minutes, until knife inserted into center comes out clean.
8. Cool on wire rack for 2 hours.
9. Serve immediately or refrigerate for later.

Note: when baking in high altitude (3,500-6,000) ft. extend second bake time to 55-60 minutes

Submitted by Christina 13, San Marcos, CA

Appendix A
Measurement Conversions

You will need some tools to use as a road map when it comes to measuring and converting between metric and traditional weights and measures.

Traditional (Imperial) Measures

3 teaspoons (tsp.) = 1 tablespoon (tbsp.)
1/4 cup = 2 ounces
1/2 cup = 4 ounces
3/4 cup = 6 ounces
1 cup = 8 ounces
2 cups = 16 ounces = 1 pint
2 pints = 32 ounces = 1 quart
2 quarts = 64 ounces = 1/2 gallon
4 quarts = 128 ounces = 1 gallon

Volume and Weight

Americans traditionally use cup measures for liquid and solid ingredients. The chart below provides a guide for converting measurements from the U.S. customary system, which is used throughout this book, to the metric system.

ml stands for milliliter
mg stands for milligram
g stands for gram
F stands for Fahrenheit
C stands for Celsius

Appendix A

Volume Equivalents

Usually when we talk about volume measurements we are talking about liquid measurements

1/4 tsp. = 1 ml
1/2 tsp. = 2 ml
1 tsp. = 5 ml
2 tsp. = 10 ml
1 tbsp. = 15 ml
1/4 cup = 60 ml
1/3 cup = 80 ml
1/2 cup = 120 ml
3/4 cup = 180 ml
1 cup = 240 ml
2 cups = 1 pint = 480 ml
4 cups = 1 qt = 950 ml

Dry Weight Equivalents

Usually when we talk about dry weight equivalents we are talking about measuring things like flour, sugar, salt etc. and it can depend on how dense what you are measuring is. For example, take the ingredients on the following page.

Notice that even though we use 1 cup as the standard, if we use grams things change a bit. Don't worry, if a recipe calls for grams they will tell you how many to use for each ingredient.

This information actually gives you a head start on your high school chemistry, how about that!

Appendix A

1 cup bread crumbs=140 grams
1 cup baking cocoa=80 grams
1 cup granulated (table) sugar=200 grams
1 cup powdered sugar=120 grams
1 cup wheat germ= 120 grams

Notice how the ingredients that seem more concentrated like cocoa and powdered sugar equal less grams?

Weight Conversions

You will most likely run across these measurements when you are using things like meat or fish in your recipes. (Please note due to fractional equivalents ounces and grams do not convert precisely.)

1 oz = 28g
2 oz = 57g
4 oz (1/4 lb) = 114g
5 oz = 142g
6 oz = 170g
8 oz (1/2 lb) = 227g
12 oz (3/4 lb) = 340g
14 oz = 397g
15 oz = 425g
16 oz (1 lb) = 450g

Appendix A

Temperature

Fahrenheit	Celsius
325	165
350	175
375	190
400	205
425	220
450	230

Again, here is a situation that probably won't occur unless you are cooking in another country or using a foreign cookbook.

If you find yourself in higher altitude than 6000 feet, you also need to adjust your cooking temperature and time. Pay attention when a recipe mentions this as failure to adjust will result in a less than stellar product and that could be embarrassing to say the least! Usually this applies to things you are baking.

Appendix B

Ingredient Substitution List

Sometimes you want to make a recipe but you don't quite have all the ingredients the recipe calls for. Here is a list of substitutions you can use instead.

1 tsp. baking powder:
    1/4 tsp. baking soda plus 5/8 tsp. cream of tartar
Or 1/4 tsp. baking soda plus 1/2 cup buttermilk

1 cup self rising flour
    1 cup sifted all-purpose flour plus 1 1/2 tsp. baking powder and 1/2 tsp. salt

1 cup all-purpose flour
    1 cup whole wheat flour
Or 1 cup whole wheat pastry flour

1 cup bread crumbs
    3/4 cup cracker crumbs

1/2 tsp. cream of tartar
    1 1/2 tsp. lemon juice or vinegar

1 tbsp. cornstarch
    2 tbsp. flour

Appendix B

Or 2 tsp. quick tapioca
Or 2 egg yolks

1 egg
    1/4 cup egg substitute

1 cup buttermilk
    1 cup plain yogurt
Or 1 tbsp. lemon juice stirred into milk to make 1 cup; let stand 5 minutes
    (never use milk that has been in the frig too long and is sour; its spoiled)

1 cup sour cream
    1 cup plain yogurt
    3 tbsp. melted butter stirred into 7/8 cup buttermilk

1 cup ricotta cheese
    1 cup cottage cheese

1 cup butter
    1 cup margarine
Or 7/8 cup vegetable oil
Or 7/8 cup butter flavored shortening

1 cup vegetable oil
    1 cup applesauce

Appendix B

1 lb. lard
> 2 cups shortening

1 cup sugar (in baking bread)
> 1 cup honey plus a pinch of baking soda

1 cup sugar (in baking)
> $7/8$ cup honey plus a pinch of baking soda

1 cup sugar (in main dishes)
> $3/4$ cup honey

1 cup brown sugar
> 1 cup white sugar plus 2 tbsp. molasses

1 cup granulated sugar
> $1 3/4$ cups powdered sugar for uses other than baking

1 tbsp. maple sugar
> 1 tbsp. granulated sugar plus a dash of maple extract

1 cup molasses (in baking) omit baking soda; use baking powder
> 1 cup sugar

$3/4$ cup maple flavored syrup
> $3/4$ cup corn syrup

Appendix B

Or   1 cup sugar and increase liquid in recipe by 3 tbsp.

1 cup Corn syrup
> 1 1/4 cup light brown sugar plus 1/3 cup water

Or   7/8 cup honey (baked goods will brown more)

1 cup dark corn syrup
> 3/4 cup light corn syrup mixed with 1/4 light molasses

1 cup whipping cream as liquid
> 1/3 cup melted butter plus 3/4 cup milk

1 cup whipping cream, whipped
> 2 cups thawed whipped topping

Or   Chill 13 ounces evaporated milk (until ice crystals form); add 1 tsp. lemon juice, whip

1 cup light cream
> 3 tbsp. melted butter plus 3/4 cup milk

Or   1 cup evaporated milk

1 cup whole milk
: 2 tsp melted butter plus 1 cup fat-free milk or water
Or equal parts evaporated milk and water

1 cup sweetened condensed milk
: Dissolve 1 cup plus 2 tbsp. dry milk powder plus 1/2 cup warm water plus 3/4 cup sugar

1 cup Coconut cream
: 1 cup whipping cream

1 large marshmallow
: 10 minis

1 ounce unsweetened chocolate
: 1 square or 3 tbsp. unsweetened cocoa powder plus 1 tbsp. butter

6 squares or 6 ounces semisweet chocolate, melted
: 1 cup semisweet chocolate chips, melted

Semi sweet chocolate
: 1 ounce unsweetened chocolate plus 4 tsp. sugar

Unsweetened chocolate
: 3 tbsp. unsweetened cocoa plus 1 tbsp. butter

1 tsp. pumpkin pie spice
> 1/4 tsp. nutmeg, 1/4 tsp. ginger, 1/2 tsp. cinnamon

1 tsp. lemon juice
> 1/2 tsp. vinegar

1 tbsp. fresh herbs
> 1/2 to 1 tsp. dry herbs

1 clove garlic
> 1/8 tsp. garlic powder

½ cup dry wine
> 2 tbsp. sherry or port

1 tsp. dry mustard
> 1 tbsp. prepared mustard
Or 1/2 tsp. mustard seed

1 pound tomatoes
> 3 medium
Or 3/4 cup sauce (6 ounces)
Or 1/4 cup tomato paste (2 ounces)

8 ounces tomato sauce
> 2/3 cup water plus 1/3 cup tomato paste

3 cups tomato juice
> 2 1/2 cups water plus 6 ounces tomato paste plus 3/4 tsp. salt and dash of sugar

Index

A
A Quiz to Get You Started 10
About the Artist 131
About The Author 130
Acknowledgements i
Appendix A 114
Appendix B 118
Apple Crisp 61
Applesauce 63
Apple Salad, Sassy 64
Apples, Baked 53

B
Bailey's Grilled Salmon Caesar Salad 74
Baked Apples 53
Banana Bread, Liberty's Favorite 33
Banana Nut Loaf, Warp Speed 39
Bananarama Shake 23
Berry Delight 24
Blueberry Hazelnut Muffins 38
Burrito, Ham and Cheese 48

C
Cake, Hawaiian Pineapple 110
Cake, Wonderfully Chocolate 108
California Chicken Salad 66
Cheese and Veggie Scramble 18
Chicken, Crock Pot Mushroom 91
Chicken Nuggets, Crunchy 88
Chicken Salad, California 66
Chicken, Spinach, & Fruit Salad 69

Index

Chile Relleno Casserole 93
Chile, Taco 81
Chili, Lightning Speed, 5 can 80
Chocolate Glaze 109
Christina's Basic Chicken Noodle Soup 77
Coffee Cake, Oatmeal and Apple 34
Cookies, Pumpkin 105
Crazy Corn 51
Cream Cheese Roll Up 47
Cream Cheese Topping, Lite 111
Cream Glaze 109
Creamy Pumpkin Soup 76
Create Your Own Omelette 17
Cremesickle, Orange/Banana 26
Crock Pot Mushroom Chicken 91
Crunchy Chicken Nuggets 88

D

Disclaimer Page 8
Dressing:Bailey's Grilled Salmon Caesar Salad .. 75
Dressing:Chicken Spinach and Fruit 69
Dressing:Lentil and Rice Salad 73
Dry weight Equivalents 115

E

Easy Black Bean Soup 78
Easy Cheesy Popcorn 52
Easy Pinwheels 40
Easy Strawberry Ice Cream 104
EggMcposerMuffin 16

Index

F
Fettuccini Alfredo 86
Fettuccini Alfredo on the Lighter Side 87
Fitness Muffins 37
French Fries, No Guilt 99
French Toast 21
Frittata, Zesty Zucchini 95

G
Garlic Toast 103
Glaze, Chocolate 109
Glaze, Cream 109
Good Old Pumpkin Pie 113
Guacamole, Wholey 59

H
Ham and Cheese Burrito 48
Hawaiian Pineapple Cake 110
Helpful Kitchen Tips 13
Herbed Potato Salad 71

I
Ice Cream, Easy Strawberry 104
Ingredient Substitution List 118
Introduction to Parents 1
Introduction to Tweens 6
Italian Tomato and Basil Pasta 85

L
Liberty's Favorite Banana Bread 33
Lightning Speed, , 5 Can Chili 80
Lentil & Rice Salad 72
Lite Cream Cheese Topping 111

Index

M
Make Your Own Sprouts 46
Mom's Hearty Split Pea Soup 79
Muffins, Blueberry Hazelnut 38
Muffins, Fitness 37

N
No Guilt French Fries 99

O
Oatmeal and Applesauce Coffee Cake 34
Omelette, Create Your Own 17
Orange/Banana Cremesickle 26

P
Pancakes, Quick & Easy Cottage Cheese 20
Pasta, Italian Tomato and Basil 85
Peanut Bread, Quick 35
Peanut Butter and Banana Toast 32
Personal Pizza 49
Pie, Good Old Pumpkin 113
Pinwheels, Easy 40
Popcorn, Easy Cheesy 52
Potato Salad, Herbed 71
Potatoes, Stuffed Cheesy 100
Pumpkin Cookies 105
Pumpkin Pie, Good Old 113
Pumpkin Soup, Creamy 76
Pumpkin Spice Shake 27

Index

Q
Quesadilla 54
Quick & Easy Cottage Cheese Pancakes 20
Quick Herbed Rice 101
Quick Peanut Bread 35

R
Red, Yellow and Green Veggie Medley 102
References 132
Rice, Quick Herbed 101
Ricotta Pear Broil 43

S
Salad, Bailey's Grilled Salmon Caesar 74
Salad, California Chicken 66
Salad, Chicken, Spinach & Fruit 69
Salad, Herbed Potato 71
Salad, Lentil and Rice 72
Salad, Sumi 65
Salad, Three Bean 68
Sassy Apple Salad 64
Sawyer's Shrimp Scampi 84
Shrimp Scampi, Sawyer's 84
Soup, Christina's Basic Chicken Noodle 77
Soup, Creamy Pumpkin 76
Soup, Easy Black Bean 78
Some General Words 11
Soup, Mom's Hearty Split Pea 79
Stevia 25
Stuffed Cheesy Potatoes 100
Sumi Salad 65
Sweet Potato, Garlic and Apple Skillet 96

Index

T
Table of Contents ii
Taco Chile 81
Temperature 117
Three Bean Salad 68
Tofu and Veggie Stir-Fry 82
Tropical Delight 31
Tuna Stuffed Pita 45

U
UFO's 19

V
Vegetarian Wrap 41
Veggie Bites 55
Veggie Medley, Red, Yellow and Green 102
Volume Equivalents 115
Volume and Weight 114

W
Warp Speed Banana Nut Loaf 39
Weight Conversions 116
Wholey Guacamole! 59
Wonderfully Chocolate Cake 108

Y
You Go…YOGO 29

Z
Zucchini, Zesty Frittata 95

About the Author

Corie Goodson MPH, CHES has been talking to people about health for as long as she can remember. After earning a Bachelor's of Science in Community Health Education, she worked as a health educator. Her job was to teach clients how to turn their health around through diet and lifestyle after they had already become sick. Unfortunately, trying to fix what had already been broken was extremely frustrating.

She went on to get her Master's in Public Health to teach prevention at the community college level, hoping that knowledge would help people become healthier as they aged. Again, the reality was that she could only capture a very small fraction of the population with this effort.

With children's health being such an important and timely issue she decided to change her focus. She became a health promotion speaker, doing seminars wherever people would listen. That is where the idea for this book was born. Tween Kwisine: *A Road to Better Health* is intended to be a fun interactive way to instill health education and be entertaining as well as reintroduce the joy of cooking to our kids.

Corie believes that kids should enjoy the food they are creating and eating and that moderation not deprivation promotes a more consistent pattern over a lifetime. Kids provide the perfect palate for learning and change. Teaching them the importance of nutrition at an early age will help them live the healthiest lives possible.

About the Artist

Julie Malfitano grew up at the base of the Rocky Mountains in Longmont, Colorado. From the instant she could hold a pencil Julie has dedicated every spare moment drawing anything and everything that came to mind. Her favorite subjects have always been whimsical cartoon characters and fairytale creatures, but she also adores painting classical portraits of children and families in natural settings.

Julie had always planned to pursue a career as a commercial artist and in 1996 she graduated from The Art Center of Albuquerque with a degree in Advertising Art. Because of her diversity and ability to render art in numerous mediums and styles, she became very successful but eventually became stifled by the nature of the business and longed for more creative freedom and flexibility.

In the year 2001 with the loving support of her husband, she left advertising behind and began working as a freelance portrait artist and illustrator where she could freely express herself and spend more time with her family. Despite the cut in income and a few lifestyle adjustments, it is a decision Julie has never regretted. Every day brings new adventures carried on the wings of her two beautiful children who constantly inspire her and her loving husband who never stops believing in her.

References

About Southern U.S. Cuisine, "Ingredient Substitution List" 2004

American Cancer Society, 2004

Archives of Pediatric & Adolescent Medicine, 1996; 150: 81-86

Archives of Pediatric & Adolescent Medicine, 2000; 54: 203-287

Berenson, Gerald, "Epidemiology of Essential Hypertension in Children" Pediatric Hypertension. Bogalusa Heart Study: June, 2004; 121-142

Bogalusa Heart Study; National Heart Lung and Blood Institute (NHLBI) 2002

International Journal of Obesity, 1999; 23 (supp2) S2-S11

Journal of the American Dietetic Association, 1999

National Safety Associates; Children's Research Foundation: 12 month trial results, 2004

Pediatrics 1998; 101 (3) 497-504

That's My Home "Ingredient Substitution List" 2004

Some of the food history and facts were contributed by: Margen, S., & "Eds." of The University of California at Berkeley WELLNESS LETTER. (1992) *The Wellness Encyclopedia of Food and Nutrition: How to Buy, Store, & Prepare Every Variety of Fresh Food..* New York: Random House.

Printed in the United States
60115LVS00002B/148-165